To.........................

From......................

Purple Ronnie's

Little Book to say

I ♥ MUM

lovely → mum

First published 2011 by Boxtree

an imprint of Pan Macmillan, a division of Macmillan Publishers Limited

Pan Macmillan, 20 New Wharf Road, London N1 9RR

Basingstoke and Oxford

Associated companies throughout the world

www.panmacmillan.com

ISBN 978 0 7522 2725 2

9 8 7 6 5 4 3 2 1

A CIP catalogue record for this book is
available from the British Library.

Printed and bound in Hong Kong

'Purple Ronnie' created by Giles Andreae. The right of Giles Andreae and Janet Cronin
to be identified respectively as the author and illustrator of this work has been asserted by them
in accordance with the Copyright, Designs and Patents Act 1988.

Visit **www.panmacmillan.com** to read more about all our books
and to buy them. You will also find features, author interviews and
news of any author events, and you can sign up for e-newsletters
so that you're always first to hear about our new releases.

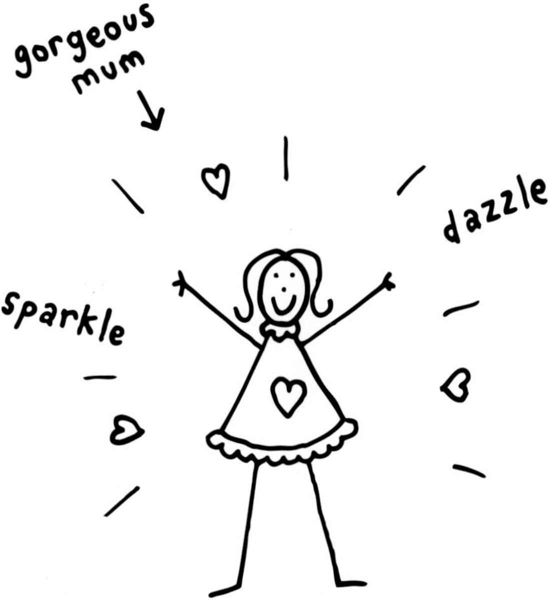
gorgeous mum
dazzle
sparkle

a poem about the

Best Mum in the World

The trumpets give a fanfare

The banner is unfurled

Just which mother are you?

THE BEST MUM IN THE ♡ WORLD!!! ♡

a poem about my

Best Mate

If I have a problem
With a boyfriend or a date
I talk to Mum about it
As she's my bestest mate

Charity Shop Trawlers

Some mums love a bargain

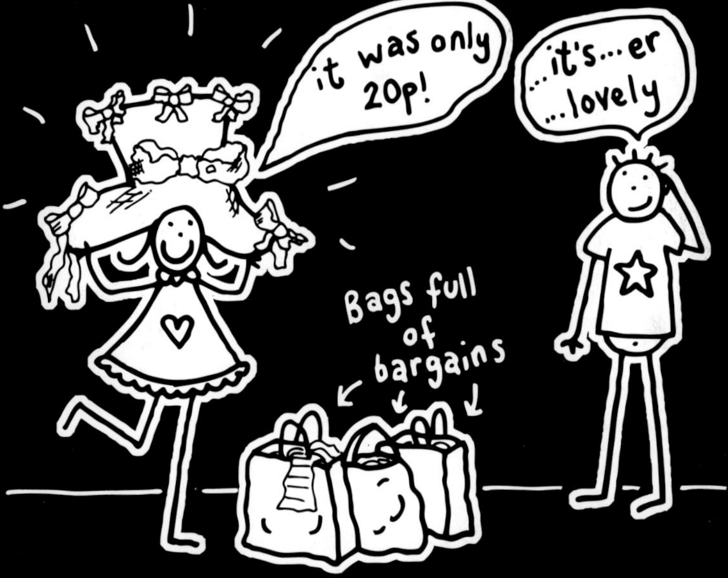
it was only 20p!
...it's...er ...lovely
Bags full of bargains

a poem about

Mums and Chores

Housework can be such
a drag
And clearing up just bores
But someone's got to do it –
So help Mum with the
chores

Makeover Mums

Some mums like to rearrange the furniture

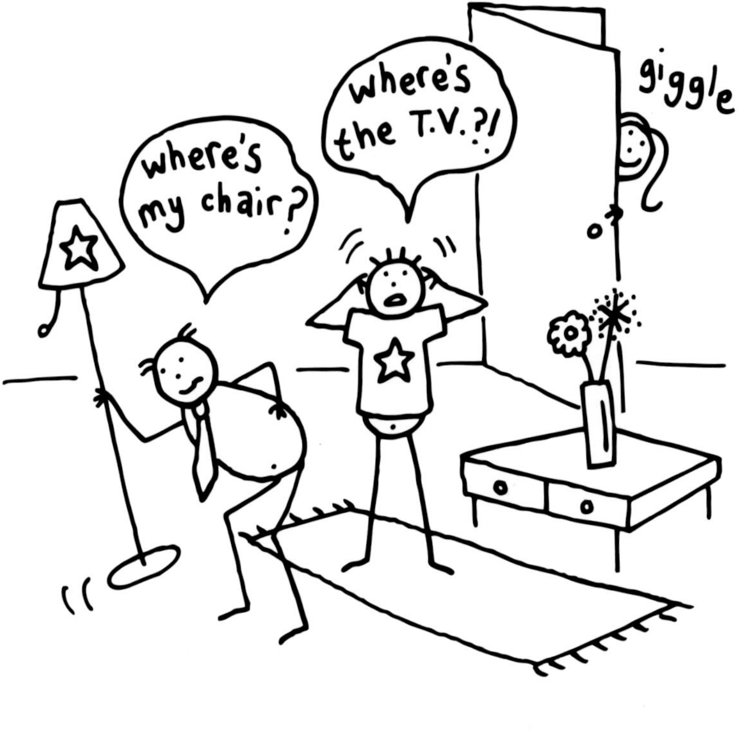
where's my chair?
where's the T.V.?!
giggle

a poem about

Posh Mums

Mums may seem so very
posh,
A classy breed apart.
But, trust me, even posh
mums
Are sometimes heard to
fart!

Champion Hampers

Mums pack amazing picnics

There's jammy buns, peanut and banana surprise, pickled egg, egg mayo, eggy flan, cheese and pickle, jellyrolls blah blah
bottom-less hamper
hee hee
yummy!
Pop

boom!
Don't even think about leaving those trainers in here!!
blast!
gulp
drop
whiff

a poem about

Tiny Mums

A mum may look quite
tiny.

But, even so, watch out.

A tiny mum when rattled

Can really raise a shout!

Relative Experts

Mums are experts
in family history

... here you go, have a nice cup of tea, she was never good enough for you
thanks Mum
You're chuck -ed

a poem about a

Caring Mum

She brings you tea and sympathy

She brings you tea and toast

There's no-one cares so much
for you

As Mum, who cares the
most

Practical Mums

Mums are often good
at sorting things out

a poem about

Gardening Mum

Some mums like to cook alot

Some mums read for hours

My Mum loves her garden

Just look at all the flowers!

a poem about

Mum the Cook

What's that scrumptious
                smell there?

I've got to take a look

Oh, yummy munch! It's Sunday
                        Lunch

By Mum, the world's best
                    cook!

a poem about

Lovely Mum

Babes come young and sassy
But some of them are dumb
Who's always bright and
                beautiful?
Who else? My lovely Mum!

Pampering Mum

Every mum deserves to be spoiled a bit sometimes

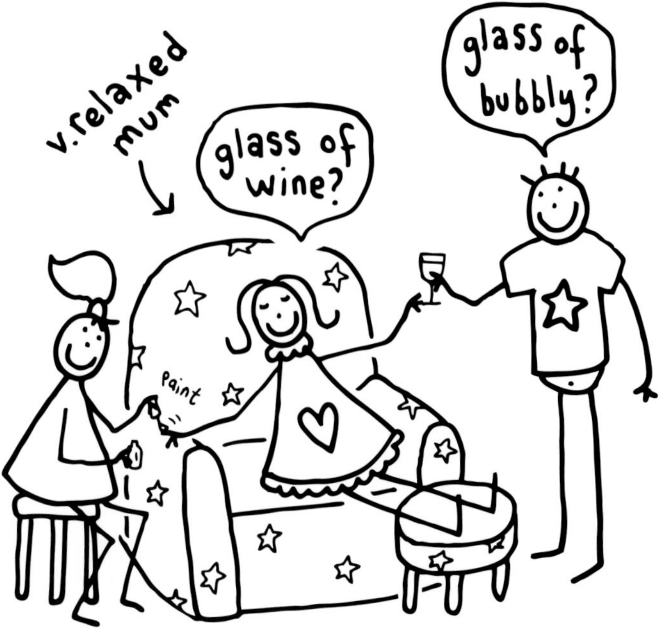
v.relaxed mum
glass of wine?
glass of bubbly?
paint

Talkative Mums

Some mums talk to everyone and anyone

He's ever so good with computers...
blush
!
tap
?
SPORT NEWS
No Balls
rubbish
BUS STOP

a poem about

Mum's Dancing

Mum should be more dignified
I'M the teenage child
But when I put my music on —
Blimey! Mum goes wild!

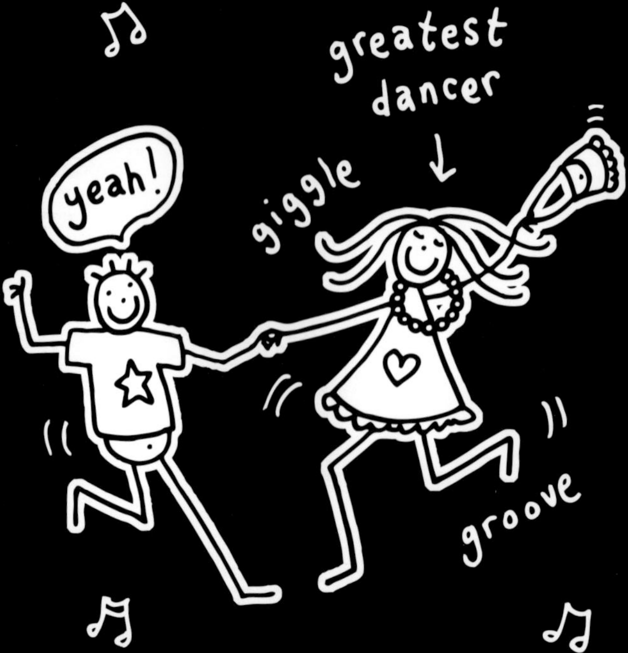
yeah!
giggle
greatest dancer
groove

a poem about my

Groovy Mum

Some say mums get frumpy
It may be sometimes true
But my Mum's really funky
Just look at her...Wahoo!

Family Albums

Mums often like to think of the past

ooh, he was a lovely little boy when he had his curls
oh cute!
suffering in silence

Mums Go Glam

Some mums like to glam up for special occasions.

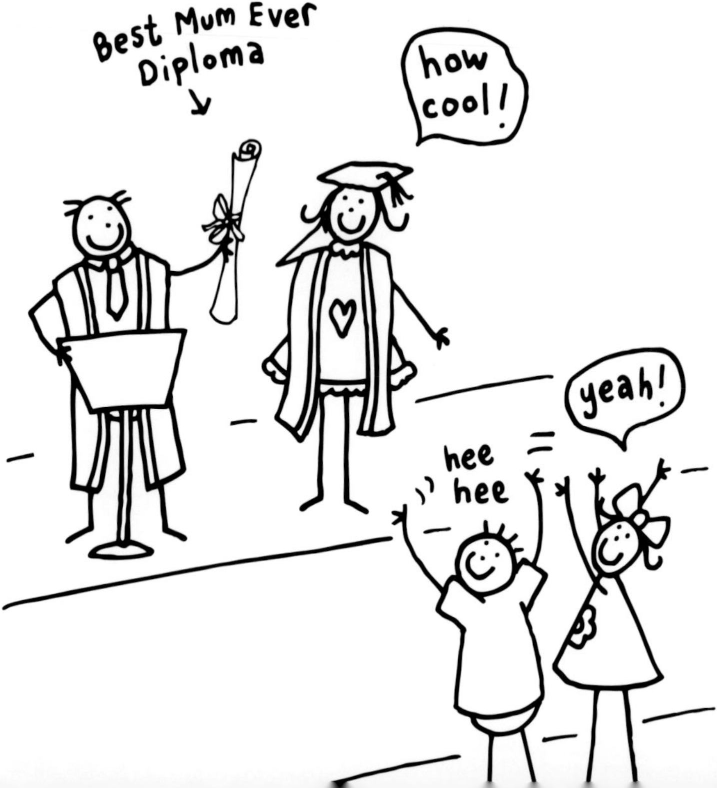
Best Mum Ever Diploma
how cool!
yeah!
hee hee

a poem about a

Top Mum

If mums did tricky Mum
Exams
And my Mum sat the test
I'll bet that lovely dear
old girl
Would come out top –
The Best !

a poem about

Soppy Mums

When Mum comes to the
movies
Bring tissues - don't forget
She cries at happy endings

And can she cry? You bet!

Kitchen Wizard Mums

Mums can knock up a meal from scratch

a poem about

Mum and Me

There's nothing like a
sit down
With a nice hot cup of
tea
Especially when it's
just us two,
My dear old Mum and me

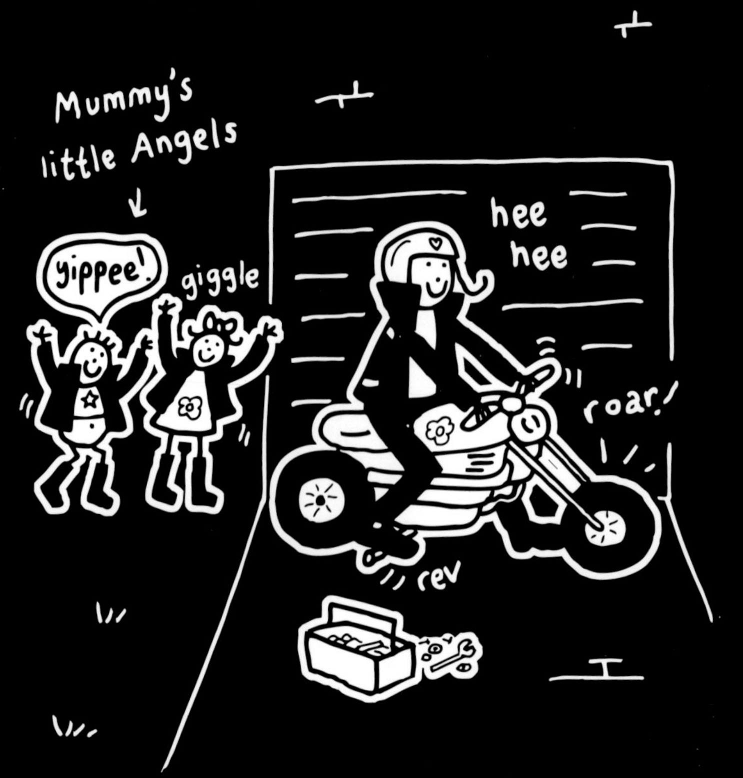
Mummy's little Angels
yippee!
giggle
hee hee
roar!
rev

a poem about an

Angel Mum

My Mum's a real Angel
But not the kind you'd like
She puts on greasy leathers
And rides a motorbike!

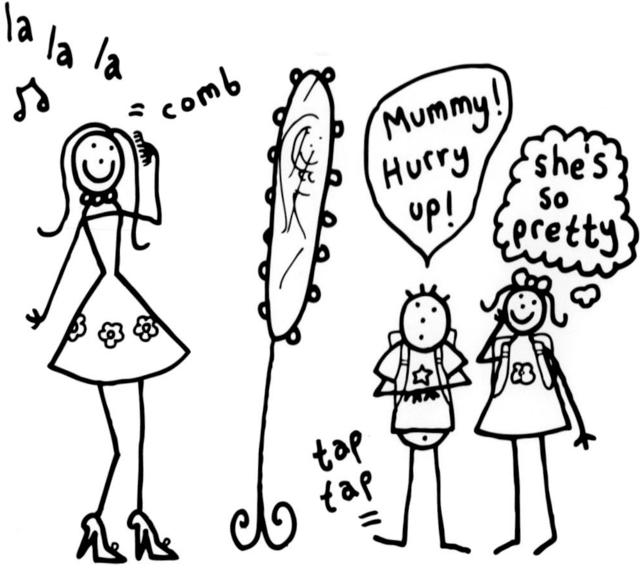
la la la
= comb
Mummy! Hurry up!
she's so pretty
tap tap

a poem about a

Yummy Mummy

Pushing up her lovely boobs

Pulling in her tummy

She wants to look her very
best

'Cos she's a Yummy Mummy!

Mystical Mums

Mums often know how you are without being told

a poem about

My Mum

Partners sometimes dump you

And mates can let you down

So in the end your truest
friend

Is Mum--- she wears the
crown

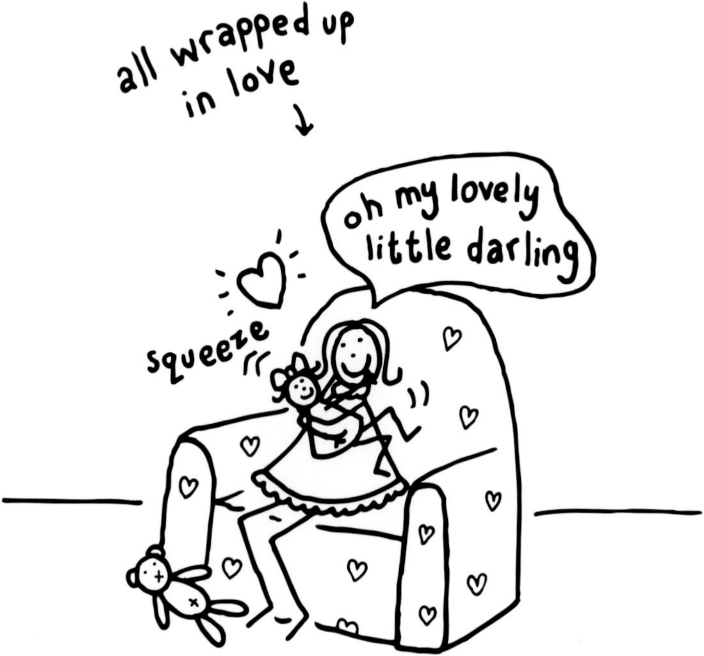
all wrapped up in love
oh my lovely little darling
squeeze

a poem about

Mummy Hugs

When I was just a baby
I loved my dolls and dummy
But best of all my comforts
Was a lovely hug from
Mummy!

a poem to say

I Love Mum

What to say on Mother's Day?
Come on, don't be dumb

It's not that hard to
sign a card
Announcing: I LOVE MUM!!!